Kora in Hell

Improvisations

William Carlos Williams

Alpha Editions

This edition published in 2022

ISBN : 9789356574502

Design and Setting By
Alpha Editions
www.alphaedis.com
Email - info@alphaedis.com

As per information held with us this book is in Public Domain.
This book is a reproduction of an important historical work. Alpha Editions uses the best technology to reproduce historical work in the same manner it was first published to preserve its original nature. Any marks or number seen are left intentionally to preserve its true form.

PROLOGUE

THE RETURN OF THE SUN

> Her voice was like rose-fragrance waltzing in the wind.
>
> She seemed a shadow, stained with shadow colors,
>
> Swimming through waves of sunlight.…

The sole precedent I can find for the broken style of my prologue is Longinus on the Sublime and that one far-fetched.

When my mother was in Rome on that rare journey forever to be remembered, she lived in a small pension near the Pincio gardens. The place had been chosen by my brother as one notably easy of access, being in a quarter free from confusion of traffic, on a street close to the park and furthermore the tram to the American Academy passed at the corner. Yet never did my mother go out but she was in fear of being lost. By turning to the left when she should have turned right, actually she did once manage to go so far astray that it was nearly an hour before she extricated herself from the strangeness of every new vista and found a landmark.

There has always been a disreputable man of picturesque personality associated with this lady. Their relations have been marked by the most rollicking spirit of comradeship. Now it has been William, former sailor in Admiral Dewey's fleet at Manila, then Tom O'Rourck who has come to her to do odd jobs and to be cared for more or less when drunk or ill, their Penelope. William would fall from the grapearbor much to my mother's amusement and delight and to his blustering discomfiture or he would stagger to the back door nearly unconscious from bad whiskey. There she would serve him with very hot and very strong coffee, then put him to scrubbing the kitchen floor into his suddy-pail pouring half a bottle of ammonia which would make the man gasp and water at the eyes as he worked and became sober.

She has always been incapable of learning from benefit or disaster. If a man cheat her she will remember that man with a violence that I have seldom seen equaled but so far as that could have an influence on her judgment of the next man or woman, she might be living in Eden. And indeed she is, an impoverished, ravished Eden but one indestructible as the imagination itself. Whatever is before her is sufficient to itself and so to be valued. Her meat though more delicate in fiber is of a kind with that of Villon and La Grosse Margot:

>Vente, gresle, gelle, j'ai mon pain cuit!

Carl Sandburg sings a negro cotton picker's song of the bol weevil. Verse after verse tells what they would do to the insect. They propose to place it in the sand, in hot ashes, in the river, and other unlikely places but the bol weevil's refrain is always: "That'll be ma HOME! That'll be ma HOOME!"

My mother is given over to frequent periods of great depression being as I believe by nature the most light-hearted thing in the world. But there comes a grotesque turn to her talk, a macabre anecdote concerning some dream, a passionate statement about death, which elevates her mood without marring it, sometimes in a most startling way.

Looking out at our parlor window one day I said to her: "We see all the shows from here, don't we, all the weddings and funerals?" (They had been preparing a funeral across the street, the undertaker was just putting on his overcoat.) She replied: "Funny profession that, burying the dead people. I should think they wouldn't have any delusions of life left." W.—Oh yes, it's merely a profession. M.—Hm. And how they study it! They say sometimes people look terrible and they come and make them look fine. They push things into their mouths! (Realistic gesture) W.—Mama! M.—Yes, when they haven't any teeth.

By some such dark turn at the end she raises her story out of the commonplace: "Look at that chair, look at it! (The plasterers had just left) If Mrs. J. or Mrs. D. saw that they would have a fit." W.—Call them in, maybe it will kill them. M.—But they're not near as bad as that woman, you know, her husband was in the chorus,—has a little daughter Helen. Mrs. B. yes. She once wanted to take rooms here. I didn't want her. They told me: 'Mrs. Williams, I heard you're going to have Mrs. B. *She* is particular.' She said so herself. Oh no! Once she burnt all her face painting under the sink.

Thus seeing the thing itself without forethought or afterthought but with great intensity of perception my mother loses her bearings or associates with some disreputable person or translates a dark mood. She is a creature of great imagination. I might say this is her sole remaining quality. She is a despoiled, moulted castaway but by this power she still breaks life between her fingers.

Once when I was taking lunch with Walter Arensberg at a small place on 63rd St. I asked him if he could state what the more modern painters were about, those roughly classed at that time as "cubists": Gleisze, Man

Ray, Demuth, Du Champs—all of whom were then in the city. He replied by saying that the only way man differed from every other creature was in his ability to improvise novelty and, since the pictorial artist was under discussion, anything in paint that is truly new, truly a fresh creation is good art. Thus according to Du Champs, who was Arensberg's champion at the time, a stained glass window that had fallen out and lay more or less together on the ground was of far greater interest than the thing conventionally composed *in situ*.

We returned to Arensberg's sumptuous studio where he gave further point to his remarks by showing me what appeared to be the original of Du Champs' famous, Nude Descending a Staircase. But this, he went on to say, is a full-sized photographic print of the first picture with many new touches by Du Champs himself and so by the technique of its manufacture as by other means it is a novelty!

Led on by these enthusiasms Arensberg has been an indefatigable worker for the yearly salon of the Society of Independent Artists, Inc. I remember the warmth of his description of a pilgrimage to the home of that old Boston hermit who watched over by a forbidding landlady (evidently in his pay) paints the cigar-box-cover-like nudes upon whose fingers he presses actual rings with glass jewels from the five and ten cent store.

I wish Arensberg had my opportunity for prying into jaded households where the paintings of Mama's and Papa's flowertime still hang on the walls. I propose that Arensberg be commissioned by the Independent Artists to scour the country for the abortive paintings of those men and women who without master or method have evolved perhaps two or three unusual creations in their early years. I would start the collection with a painting I have by a little English woman, A. E. Kerr, 1906, that in its unearthly gaiety of flowers and sobriety of design possesses exactly that strange freshness a spring day approaches without attaining, an expansion of April, a thing this poor woman found too costly for her possession—she could not swallow it as the niggers do diamonds in the mines. Carefully selected these queer products might be housed to good effect in some unpretentious exhibition chamber across the city from the Metropolitan Museum of Art. In the anteroom could be hung perhaps photographs of prehistoric rock-paintings and etchings on horn: galloping bisons and stags, the hind feet of which have been caught by the artist in such a position that from that time until the invention of the camera obscura, a matter of 6000 years or more, no one on earth had again depicted that most delicate and expressive posture of running.

The amusing controversy between Arensberg and Du Champs on one side, and the rest of the hanging committee on the other as to whether the porcelain urinal was to be admitted to the Palace Exhibition of 1917 as a representative piece of American Sculpture should not be allowed to slide into oblivion.

One day Du Champs decided that his composition for that day would be the first thing that struck his eye in the first hardware store he should enter. It turned out to be a pickaxe which he bought and set up in his studio. This was his composition. Together with Mina Loy and a few others Du Champs and Arensberg brought out the paper, The Blind Man, to which Robert Carlton Brown with his vision of suicide by diving from a high window of the Singer Building contributed a few poems.

In contradistinction to their south, Marianne Moore's statement to me at the Chatham parsonage one afternoon—my wife and I were just on the point of leaving—sets up a north: My work has come to have just one quality of value in it: I will not touch or have to do with those things which I detest. In this austerity of mood she finds sufficient freedom for the play she chooses.

Of all those writing poetry in America at the time she was here Marianne Moore was the only one Mina Loy feared. By divergent virtues these two women have achieved freshness of presentation, novelty, freedom, break with banality.

When Margaret Anderson published my first improvisations Ezra Pound wrote me one of his hurried letters in which he urged me to give some hint by which the reader of good will might come at my intention.

Before Ezra's permanent residence in London, on one of his trips to America—brought on I think by an attack of jaundice—he was glancing through some book of my father's. "It is not necessary," he said, "to read everything in a book in order to speak intelligently of it. Don't tell everybody I said so," he added.

During this same visit my father and he had been reading and discussing poetry together. Pound has always liked my father. "I of course like your Old Man and I have drunk his Goldwasser." They were hot for an argument that day. My parent had been holding forth in downright sentences upon my own "idle nonsense" when he turned and became equally vehement concerning something Ezra had written: what in heaven's name Ezra meant by "jewels" in a verse that had come between them. These jewels,—rubies, sapphires, amethysts and what not, Pound went on to explain with great determination and care, were the backs of books as they stood on a man's shelf. "But why in heaven's name don't you say so then?" was my father's triumphant and crushing rejoinder.

The letter: … God knows I have to work hard enough to escape, not *propagande*, but getting centered in *propagande*. And America? What the h—l do you a blooming foreigner know about the place. Your *père* only penetrated the edge, and you've never been west of Upper Darby, or the Maunchunk switchback.

Would H., with the swirl of the prairie wind in her underwear, or the Virile Sandburg recognize you, an effete easterner as a REAL American? INCONCEIVABLE!!!!!

My dear boy you have never felt the woop of the PEEraries. You have never seen the projecting and protuberant Mts. of the SIerra Nevada. WOT can you know of the country?

You have the naive credulity of a Co. Claire emigrant. But I (der grosse Ich) have the virus, the bacillus of the land in my blood, for nearly three bleating centuries.

(Bloody snob. 'eave a brick at 'im!!!)….

I was very glad to see your wholly incoherent unamerican poems in the L. R.

Of course Sandburg will tell you that you miss the "big drifts," and Bodenheim will object to your not being sufficiently decadent.

You thank your bloomin gawd you've got enough Spanish blood to muddy up your mind, and prevent the current American ideation from going through it like a blighted collander.

The thing that saves your work is opacity, and don't forget it. Opacity is NOT an American quality. Fizz, swish, gabble, and verbiage, these are *echt Americanisch*.

And alas, alas, poor old Masters. Look at Oct. Poetry.

Let me indulge the American habit of quotation:

"Si le cosmopolitisme littéraire gagnait encore et qu'il réussit à étaindre ce que les différence de race ont allumé de haine de sang parmi les hommes, j'y verrais un gain pour la civilization et pour l'humanité tout entière"….

"L'amour excessif d'une patrie a pour immédiat corollair l'horreur des patries étrangères. Non seulment on craint de quitter la jupe de sa maman, d'aller voir comment vivent les autres hommes, de se mêler à leur luttes, de partager leur travaux, non seulment on reste chez soi, mais on finit par fermer sa porte."

"Cette folie gagne certains littérateurs et le même professeur, en sortant d'expliquer le Cid ou Don Juan, rédige de gracieuses injures contre Ibsen et l'influence, hélas, trop illusoire, de son oevre, pourtant toute de lumière et de beauté." et cetera. Lie down and compose yourself.

I like to think of the Greeks as setting out for the colonies in Sicily and the Italian Peninsula. The Greek temperament lent itself to a certain symmetrical sculptural phase and to a fat poetical balance of line that produced important work but I like better the Greeks setting their backs to Athens. The ferment was always richer in Rome, the dispersive explosion was always nearer, the influence carried further and remained hot longer. Hellenism, especially the modern sort, is too staid, too chilly, too little fecundative to impregnate my world.

Hilda Doolittle before she began to write poetry or at least before she began to show it to anyone would say: "You're not satisfied with me, are you Billy? There's something lacking, isn't there?" When I was with her my feet always seemed to be sticking to the ground while she would be walking on the tips of the grass stems.

Ten years later as assistant editor of the Egoist she refers to my long poem, March, which thanks to her own and her husband's friendly attentions finally appeared there in a purified form:

14 Aug. 1916

Dear Bill:—

I trust you will not hate me for wanting to delete from your poem all the flippancies. The reason I want to do this is that the beautiful lines are so very beautiful—so in the tone and spirit of your *Postlude*—(which to me stands, a Nike, supreme among your poems). I think there is *real* beauty—and real beauty is a rare and sacred thing in this generation—in all the pyramid, Ashur-ban-i-pal bits and in the Fiesole and in the wind at the very last.

I don't know what you think but I consider this business of writing a very sacred thing!—I think you have the "spark"—am sure of it, and when you speak *direct* are a poet. I feel in the hey-ding-ding touch running through your poem a derivitive tendency which, to me, is not *you*—not your very self. It is as if you were *ashamed* of your Spirit, ashamed of your inspiration!—as if you mocked at your own song. It's very well to *mock* at yourself—it is a spiritual sin to mock at your inspiration—

Hilda.

Oh well, all this might be very disquieting were it not that "sacred" has lately been discovered to apply to a point of arrest where stabilization has gone on past the time. There is nothing sacred about literature, it is damned from one end to the other. There is nothing in literature but change and change is mockery. I'll write whatever I damn please, whenever I damn please and as I damn please and it'll be good if the authentic spirit of change is on it.

But in any case H. D. misses the entire intent of what I am doing no matter how just her remarks concerning that particular poem happen to have been. The hey-ding-ding touch *was* derivitive but it filled a gap that I did not know how better to fill at the time. It might be said that that touch is the prototype of the improvisations.

It is to the inventive imagination we look for deliverance from every other misfortune as from the desolation of a flat Hellenic perfection of style. What good then to turn to art from the atavistic religionists, from a science doing slavey service upon gas engines, from a philosophy tangled in a miserable sort of dialect that means nothing if the full power of initiative be denied at the beginning by a lot of baying and snapping scholiasts? If the inventive imagination must look, as I think, to the field of art for its richest discoveries today it will best make its way by compass and follow no path.

But before any material progress can be accomplished there must be someone to draw a discriminating line between true and false values.

The true value is that peculiarity which gives an object a character by itself. The associational or sentimental value is the false. Its imposition is due to lack of imagination, to an easy lateral sliding. The attention has been held too rigid on the one plane instead of following a more flexible, jagged resort. It is to loosen the attention, my attention since I occupy part of the field, that I write these improvisations. Here I clash with Wallace Stevens.

The imagination goes from one thing to another. Given many things of nearly totally divergent natures but possessing one-thousandth part of a quality in common, provided that be new, distinguished, these things belong in an imaginative category and not in a gross natural array. To me this is the gist of the whole matter. It is easy to fall under the spell of a certain mode, especially if it be remote of origin, leaving thus certain of its members essential to a reconstruction of its significance permanently lost in an impenetrable mist of time. But the thing that stands eternally in the way of really good writing is always one: the virtual impossibility of lifting to the imagination those things which lie under the direct scrutiny of the senses, close to the nose. It is this difficulty that sets a value upon all works of art and makes them a necessity. The senses witnessing what is immediately before them in detail see a finality which they cling to in despair, not knowing which way to turn. Thus the so-called natural or scientific array becomes fixed, the walking devil of modern life. He who even nicks the solidity of this apparition does a piece of work superior to that of Hercules when he cleaned the Augean stables.

Stevens' letter applies really to my book of poems, "Al Que Quiere" (which means, by the way, To Him Who Wants It) but the criticism he makes of that holds good for each of the improvisations if not for the *oevre* as a whole.

It begins with a postscript in the upper left hand corner: "I think, after all, I should rather send this than not, although it is quarrelsomely full of my own ideas of discipline.

April 9

My dear Williams:

...

What strikes me most about the poems themselves is their casual character.... Personally I have a distaste for miscellany. It is one of the reasons I do not bother about a book myself.

(Wallace Stevens is a fine gentleman whom Cannell likened to a Pennsylvania Dutchman who has suddenly become aware of his habits and taken to "society" in self defence. He is always immaculately dressed. I don't know why I should always associate him in my mind with an imaginary image I have of Ford Madox Hueffer.)

...My idea is that in order to carry a thing to the extreme necessity to convey it one has to stick to it;... Given a fixed point of view, realistic, imagistic or what you will, everything adjusts itself to that point of view; and the process of adjustment is a world in flux, as it should be for a poet. But to fidget with points of view leads always to new beginnings and incessant new beginnings lead to sterility.

(This sounds like Sir Roger de Coverly)

A single manner or mood thoroughly matured and exploited is that fresh thing ... etc.

One has to keep looking for poetry as Renoir looked for colors in old walls, wood-work and so on.

Your place is

> —among children
>
> Leaping around a dead dog.

A book of that would feed the hungry....

Well a book of poems is a damned serious affair. I am only objecting that a book that contains your particular quality should contain anything else and suggesting that if the quality were carried to a communicable extreme, in intensity and volume, etc.... I see it all over the book, in your landscapes and portraits, but dissipated and obscured. Bouquets for brides and Spencerian compliments for poets.... There are a very few men who have anything native in them or for whose work I'd give a Bolshevic ruble.... But I think your tantrums not half mad enough.

(I am not quite clear about the last sentence but I presume he means that I do not push my advantage through to an overwhelming decision. What would you have me do with my Circe, Stevens, now that I have doublecrossed her game, marry her? It is not what Odysseus did).

I return Pound's letter ... observe how in everything he does he proceeds with the greatest positiveness etc.

Wallace Stevens.

I wish that I might here set down my "Vortex" after the fashion of London, 1913, stating how little it means to me whether I live here, there or elsewhere or succeed in this, that or the other so long as I can keep my mind free from the trammels of literature, beating down every attack of its *retiarii* with my *mirmillones*. But the time is past.

I thought at first to adjoin to each improvisation a more or less opaque commentary. But the mechanical interference that would result makes this inadvisable. Instead I have placed some of them in the preface where without losing their original intention (see reference numerals at the beginning of each) they relieve the later text and also add their weight to my present fragmentary argument.

V. No. 2. By the brokeness of his composition the poet makes himself master of a certain weapon which he could possess himself of in no other way. The speed of the emotions is sometimes such that thrashing about in a thin exaltation or despair many matters are touched but not held, more often broken by the contact.

II. No. 3. The instability of these improvisations would seem such that they must inevitably crumble under the attention and become particles of a wind that falters. It would appear to the unready that the fiber of the thing is a thin jelly. It would be these same fools who would deny touch cords to the wind because they cannot split a storm endwise and wrap it upon spools. The virtue of strength lies not in the grossness of the fiber but in the fiber itself. Thus a poem is tough by no quality it borrows from a logical recital of events nor from the events themselves but solely from that attenuated power which draws perhaps many broken things into a dance giving them thus a full being.

* * It is seldom that anything but the most elementary communications can be exchanged one with another. There are in reality only two or three reasons generally accepted as the causes of action. No matter what the motive it will seldom happen that true knowledge of it will be anything more than vaguely divined by some one person, some half a person whose intimacy has perhaps been cultivated over the whole of a lifetime. We live in bags. This is due to the gross fiber of all action. By action itself almost nothing can be imparted. The world of action is a world of stones.

XV. No. 1. Bla! Bla! Bla! Heavy talk is talk that waits upon a deed. Talk is servile that is set to inform. Words with the bloom on them run before the imagination like the saeter girls before Peer Gynt. It is talk with the patina of whim upon it makes action a boot-licker. So nowadays poets spit upon rhyme and rhetoric.

* * The stream of things having composed itself into wiry strands that move in one fixed direction, the poet in desperation turns at right angles and cuts across current with startling results to his hangdog mood.

XI. No. 2. In France, the country of Rabelais, they know that the world is not made up entirely of virgins. They do not deny virtue to the rest because of that. Each age has its perfections but the praise differs. It is only stupid when the praise of the gross and the transformed would be minted in unfit terms such as suit nothing but youth's sweetness and frailty. It is necessary to know that laughter is the reverse of aspiration. So they laugh well in France, at Coquelin and the *Petoman*. Their girls, also, thrive upon the love-making they get, so much so that the world runs to Paris for that reason.

XII. No. 2 B. It is chuckleheaded to desire a way through every difficulty. Surely one might even communicate with the dead—and lose his taste for truffles. Because snails are slimy when alive and because slime is associated (erroneously) with filth the fool is convinced that snails are detestable when, as it is proven every day, fried in butter with chopped parsely upon them, they are delicious. This is both sides of the question: the slave and the despoiled of his senses are one. But to weigh a difficulty and to turn it aside without being wrecked upon a destructive solution bespeaks an imagination of force sufficient to transcend action. The difficulty has thus been solved by ascent to a higher plane. It is energy of the imagination alone that cannot be laid aside.

* * Rich as are the gifts of the imagination bitterness of world's loss is not replaced thereby. On the contrary it is intensified, resembling thus possession itself. But he who has no power of the imagination cannot even know the full of his injury.

VIII. No. 3. Those who permit their senses to be despoiled of the things under their noses by stories of all manner of things removed and unattainable are of frail imagination. Idiots, it is true nothing is possessed save by dint of that vigorous conception of its perfections which is the imagination's special province but neither is anything possessed which is not extant. A frail imagination, unequal to the tasks before it, is easily led astray.

IV. No. 2. Although it is a quality of the imagination that it seeks to place together those things which have a common relationship, yet the coining of similies is a pastime of very low order, depending as it does upon a nearly vegetable coincidence. Much more keen is that power which discovers in things those inimitable particles of dissimilarity to all other things which are the peculiar perfections of the thing in question.

But this loose linking of one thing with another has effects of a destructive power little to be guessed at: all manner of things are thrown out of key so that it approaches the impossible to arrive at an understanding of anything. All is confusion, yet, it comes from a hidden desire for the dance, a lust of the imagination, a will to accord two instruments in a duet.

But one does not attempt by the ingenuity of the joiner to blend the tones of the oboe with the violin. On the contrary the perfections of the two instruments are emphasized by the joiner; no means is neglected to give to each the full color of its perfections. It is only the music of the instruments which is joined and that not by the woodworker but by the composer, by virtue of the imagination.

On this level of the imagination all things and ages meet in fellowship. Thus only can they, peculiar and perfect, find their release. This is the beneficent power of the imagination.

* * Age and youth are great flatterers. Brooding on each other's obvious psychology neither dares tell the other outright what manifestly is the truth: your world is poison. Each is secure in his own perfections. Monsieur Eichorn used to have a most atrocious body odor while the odor of some girls is a pleasure to the nostril. Each quality in each person or age, rightly valued, would mean the freeing of that age to its own delights of action or repose. Now an evil odor can be pursued with praise-worthy ardor leading to great natural activity whereas a flowery skinned virgin may and no doubt often does allow herself to fall into destructive habits of neglect.

XIII. No. 3. A poet witnessing the chicory flower and realizing its virtues of form and color so constructs his praise of it as to borrow no particle from right or left. He gives his poem over to the flower and its plant themselves that they may benefit by those cooling winds of the imagination which thus returned upon them will refresh them at their task of saving the world. But what does it mean, remarked his friends?

VII. *Coda*. It would be better than depriving birds of their song to call them all nightingales. So it would be better than to have a world stript of poetry to provide men with some sort of eyeglasses by which they should be unable to read any verse but sonnets. But fortunately although there are many sorts of fools, just as there are many birds which sing and many sorts of poems, there is no need to please them.

* * All schoolmasters are fools. Thinking to build in the young the foundations of knowledge they let slip their minds that the blocks are of grey mist bedded upon the wind. Those who will taste of the wind himself have a mark in their eyes by virtue of which they bring their masters to nothing.

* * All things brought under the hand of the possessor crumble to nothingness. Not only that: He who possesses a child if he cling to it inordinately becomes childlike, whereas, with a twist of the imagination, himself may rise into comradeship with the grave and beautiful presences of antiquity. But some have the power to free, say a young matron pursuing her infant, from her own possessions, making her kin to Yang Kuei-fei because of a haunting loveliness that clings about her knees, impeding her progress as she takes up her matronly pursuit.

* * As to the sun what is he, save for his light, more than the earth is: the same mass of metals, a mere shadow? But the winged dawn is the very essence of the sun's self, a thing cold, vitreous, a virtue that precedes the body which it drags after it.

* * The features of a landscape take their position in the imagination and are related more to their own kind there than to the country and season which has held them hitherto as a basket holds vegetables mixed with fruit.

VI. No. 1. A fish swimming in a pond, were his back white and his belly green, would be easily perceived from above by hawks against the dark depths of water and from below by larger fish against the penetrant light of the sky. But since his belly is white and his back green he swims about in safety. Observing this barren truth and discerning at once its slavish application to the exercises of the mind, a young man, who has been sitting for some time in contemplation at the edge of a lake, rejects with scorn the parochial deductions of history and as scornfully asserts his defiance.

XIV. No. 3. The barriers which keep the feet from the dance are the same which in a dream paralyze the effort to escape and hold us powerless in the track of some murderous pursuer. Pant and struggle but you cannot move. The birth of the imagination is like waking from a nightmare. Never does the night seem so beneficent.

* * The raw beauty of ignorance that lies like an opal mist over the west coast of the Atlantic, beginning at the Grand Banks and extending into the recesses of our brains—the children, the married, the unmarried—clings especially about the eyes and the throats of our girls and boys. Of a Sunday afternoon a girl sits before a mechanical piano and, working it with her hands and feet, opens her mouth and sings to the music—a popular tune, ragtime. It is a serenade. I have seen a young Frenchman lean above the piano and looking down speak gently and wonderingly to one of our girls singing such a serenade. She did not seem aware of what she was singing and he smiled an occult but thoroughly bewildered smile—as of a man waiting for a fog to lift, meanwhile lost in admiration of its enveloping beauty—fragments of architecture, a street opening and closing, a mysterious glow of sunshine.

VIII. No. 1. A man of note upon examining the poems of his friend and finding there nothing related to his immediate understanding laughingly remarked: After all, literature is communication while you, my friend, I am afraid, in attempting to do something striking, are in danger of achieving mere presciosity.——But inasmuch as the fields of the mind are vast and little explored, the poet was inclined only to smile and to take note of that hardening infirmity of the imagination which seems to endow its victim with great solidity and rapidity of judgment. But he thought to himself: And yet of what other thing is greatness composed than a power to annihilate half-truths for a thousandth part of accurate understanding. Later life has its perfections as well as that bough-bending time of the mind's florescence with which I am so discursively taken.

I have discovered that the thrill of first love passes! It even becomes the backbone of a sordid sort of religion if not assisted in passing. I knew a man who kept a candle burning before a girl's portrait day and night for a year—then jilted her, pawned her off on a friend. I have been reasonably frank about my erotics with my wife. I have never or seldom said, my dear I love you, when I would rather say: My dear, I wish you were in Tierra del Fuego. I have discovered by scrupulous attention to this detail and by certain allied experiments that we can continue from time to time to elaborate relationships quite equal in quality, if not greatly superior, to that surrounding our wedding. In fact, the best we have enjoyed of love together has come after the most thorough destruction or harvesting of that which has gone before. Periods of barrenness have intervened, periods comparable to the prison music in Fidelio or to any of Beethoven's pianissimo transition passages. It is at these times our formal relations have teetered on the edge of a debacle to be followed, as our imaginations have permitted, by a new growth of passionate attachment dissimilar in every member to that which has gone before.

It is in the continual and violent refreshing of the idea that love and good writing have their security.

Alfred Kreymborg is primarily a musician, at best an innovator of musical phrase:

> We have no dishes
>
> to eat our meals from.
>
> We have no dishes
>
> to eat our meals from
>
> because we have no dishes
>
> to eat our meals from
>
> …
>
> We need no dishes
>
> to eat our meals from,
>
> we have fingers
>
> to eat our meals from.

Kreymborg's idea of poetry is a transforming music that has much to do with tawdry things.

Few people know how to read Kreymborg. There is no modern poet who suffers more from a bastard sentimental appreciation. It is hard to get his things from the page. I have heard him say he has often thought in despair of marking his verse into measures as music is marked. Oh, well—

The man has a bare irony, the gift of rhythm and Others. I smile to think of Alfred stealing the stamps from the envelopes sent for return of MSS. to the Others office! The best thing that could happen for the good of poetry in the United States today would be for someone to give Alfred Kreymborg a hundred thousand dollars. In his mind there is the determination for freedom brought into relief by a crabbedness of temper that makes him peculiarly able to value what is being done here. Whether he is bull enough for the work I am not certain, but that he can find his way that I know.

A somewhat petulant English college friend of my brother's once remarked that Britons make the best policemen the world has ever witnessed. I agree with him. It is silly to go into a puckersnatch because some brass-button-minded nincompoop in Kensington flies off the handle and speaks openly about our United States prize poems. This Mr. Jepson— "Anyone who has heard Mr. J. read Homer and discourse on Catullus would recognize his fitness as a judge and respecter of poetry"—this is Ezra!—this champion of the right is not half a fool. His epithets and phrases—slip-shod, rank bad workmanship of a man who has shirked his job, lumbering fakement, cumbrous artificiality, maundering dribble, rancid as Ben Hur—are in the main well-merited. And besides, he comes out with one fairly lipped cornet blast: the only distinctive U. S. contributions to the arts have been ragtime and buck-dancing.

Nothing is good save the new. If a thing have novelty it stands intrinsically beside every other work of artistic excellence. If it have not that, no loveliness or heroic proportion or grand manner will save it. It will not be saved above all by an attenuated intellectuality.

But all U. S. verse is not bad according to Mr. J., there is T. S. Eliot and his, Love Song of J. Alfred Prufrock.

But our prize poems are especially to be damned not because of superficial bad workmanship, but because they are rehash, repetition—just as Eliot's more exquisite work is rehash, repetition in another way of Verlaine, Beaudelaire, Maeterlinck,—conscious or unconscious,—just as there were Pound's early paraphrases from Yeats and his constant later cribbing from the renaissance, Provence and the modern French: Men content with the connotations of their masters.

It is convenient to have fixed standards of comparison: All antiquity! And there is always some everlasting Polonius of Kensington forever to rate highly his eternal Eliot. It is because Eliot is a subtle conformist. It tickles the palate of this archbishop of procurers to a lecherous antiquity to hold up Prufrock as a New World type. Prufrock, the nibbler at sophistication, endemic in every capital, the not quite (because he refuses to turn his back), is "the soul of that modern land," the United States!

> Blue undershirts,
>
> Upon a line,
>
> It is not secessary to say to you
>
> Anything about it—

I cannot question Eliot's observation. Prufrock is a masterly portrait of the man just below the summit, but the type is universal; the model in his case might be Mr. J.

No. The New World is Montezuma or since he was stoned to death in a parley, Guatemozin who had the city of Mexico levelled over him before he was taken.

For the rest, there is no man even though he dare who can make beauty his own and "so at last live," at least there is no man better situated for that achievement than another. As Prufrock longed for his silly lady so Kensington longs for its Hardanger dairymaid. By a mere twist of the imagination, if Prufrock only knew it, the whole world can be inverted (why else are there wars?) and the mermaids be set warbling to whoever will listen to them. Seesaw and blind-man's-buff converted into a sort of football.

But the summit of United States achievement, according to Mr. J.—who can discourse on Catullus—is that very beautiful poem of Eliot's, La Figlia Que Piange: just the right amount of everything drained through, etc., etc., etc., etc., the rhythm delicately studied and—IT CONFORMS! ergo here we have "the very fine flower of the finest spirit of the United States."

Examined closely this poem reveals a highly refined distillation. Added to the already "faithless" formula of yesterday we have a conscious simplicity:

> Simple and faithless as a smile and shake of the hand.

The perfection of that line is beyond cavil. Yet, in the last stanza, this paradigm, this very fine flower of U. S. art is warped out of alignment, obscured in meaning even to the point of an absolute unintelligibility by the inevitable straining after a rhyme, the very cleverness with which this straining is covered being a sinister token in itself.

And I wonder how they should have been together!

So we have no choice but to accept the work of this fumbling conjurer.

Upon the Jepson filet Eliot balances his mushroom. It is the latest touch from the literary cuisine, it adds to the pleasant outlook from the club window. If to do this, if to be a Whistler at best, in the art of poetry, is to reach the height of poetic expression then Ezra and Eliot have approached it and *tant pis* for the rest of us.

The Adobe Indian hag sings her lullaby:

> The beetle is blind
>
> The beetle is blind
>
> The beetle is blind
>
> The beetle is blind, etc., etc.

and Kandinsky in his, *Ueber das Geistige in der Kunst*, sets down the following axioms for the artist:

> Every artist has to express himself
>
> Every artist has to express his epoch.
>
> Every artist has to express the pure and eternal qualities of the art of all men.

So we have the fish and the bait, but the last rule holds three hooks at once—not for the fish, however.

I do not overlook De Gourmont's plea for a meeting of the nations, but I do believe that when they meet Paris will be more than slightly abashed to find parodies of the middle ages, Dante and Langue D'Oc foisted upon it as the best in United States poetry. Even Eliot, who is too fine an artist to allow himself to be exploited by a blockheaded grammaticaster, turns recently toward "one definite false note" in his quatrains, which more nearly approach America than ever La Figlia Que Piange did. Ezra Pound is a Boscan who has met his Navagiero.

One day Ezra and I were walking down a back lane in Wyncote. I contended for bread, he for caviar. I become hot. He, with fine discretion, exclaimed: "Let us drop it. We will never agree, or come to an agreement." He spoke then like a Frenchman, which is one who discerns.

Imagine an international congress of poets at Paris or Versailles, Remy de Gourmont (now dead) presiding, poets all speaking five languages fluently. Ezra stands up to represent U. S. verse and De Gourmont sits down smiling. Ezra begins by reading, La Figlia Que Piange. It would be a pretty pastime to gather into a mental basket the fruits of that reading from the minds of the ten Frenchmen present; their impressions of the sort of United States that very fine flower was picked from. After this Kreymborg might push his way to the front and read Jack's House.

E. P. is the best enemy United States verse has. He is interested, passionately interested—even if he doesn't know what he is talking about. But of course he does know what he is talking about. He does not, however, know everything, not by more than half. The accordances of which Americans have the parts and the colors but not the completions before them pass beyond the attempts of his thought. It is a middle aging blight of the Imagination.

I praise those who have the wit and courage, and the conventionality, to go direct toward their vision of perfection in an objective world where the sign-posts are clearly marked, viz., to London. But confine them in hell for their paretic assumption that there is no alternative but their own groove.

Dear fat Stevens, thawing out so beautifully at forty! I was one day irately damning those who run to London when Stevens caught me up with his mild: "But where in the world will you have them run to?"

Nothing that I should write touching poetry would be complete without Maxwell Bodenheim in it, even had he not said that the Improvisations were "perfect," the best things I had ever done; for that I place him, Janus, first and last.

Bodenheim pretends to hate most people, including Pound and Kreymborg, but that he really goes to this trouble I cannot imagine. He seems rather to me to have the virtue of self absorbtion so fully developed that hate is made impossible. Due to this, also, he is an unbelievable physical stoic. I know of no one who lives so completely in his pretences as Bogie does. Having formulated his world neither toothache nor the misery to which his indolence reduces him can make head against the force of his imagination. Because of this he remains for me a heroic figure, which, after all, is quite apart from the stuff he writes and which only concerns him. He is an Isaiah of the butterflies.

Bogie was the young and fairly well acclaimed genius when he came to New York four years ago. He pretended to have fallen in Chicago and to have sprained his shoulder. The joint was done up in a proper Sayre's dressing and there really looked to be a bona fide injury. Of course he couldn't find any work to do with one hand so we all chipped in. It lasted a month! During that time Bogie spent a week at my house at no small inconvenience to Florence, who had two babies on her hands just then. When he left I expressed my pleasure at having had his company. "Yes," he replied, "I think you have profited by my visit." The statement impressed me by its simple accuracy as well as by the evidence it bore of that fullness of the imagination which had held the man in its tide while we had been together.

Charlie Demuth once told me that he did not like the taste of liquor, for which he was thankful, but that he found the effect it had on his mind to be delightful. Of course Li Po is reported to have written his best verse supported in the arms of the Emperor's attendants and with a dancing-girl to hold his tablet. He was also a great poet. Wine is merely the latchstring.

The virtue of it all is in an opening of the doors, though some rooms of course will be empty, a break with banality, the continual hardening which habit enforces. There is nothing left in me but the virtue of curiosity, Demuth puts in. The poet should be forever at the ship's prow.

An acrobat seldom learns really a new trick, but he must exercise continually to keep his joints free. When I made this discovery it started rings in my memory that keep following one after the other to this day.

I have placed the following Improvisations in groups, somewhat after the A. B. A. formula, that one may support the other, clarifying or enforcing perhaps the other's intention.

The arrangement of the notes, each following its poem and separated from it by a ruled line, is borrowed from a small volume of Metastasio, *Varie Poesie Dell' Abate Pietro Metastasio*, Venice, 1795.

September 1, 1918

IMPROVISATIONS

I.

1

Fools have big wombs. For the rest?—here is pennyroyal if one knows to use it. But time is only another liar, so go along the wall a little further: if blackberries prove bitter there'll be mushrooms, fairy-ring mushrooms, in the grass, sweetest of all fungi.

2

For what it's worth: Jacob Louslinger, white haired, stinking, dirty bearded, cross eyed, stammer tongued, broken voiced, bent backed, ball kneed, cave bellied, mucous faced—deathling,—found lying in the weeds "up there by the cemetery". "Looks to me as if he'd been bumming around the meadows for a couple of weeks". Shoes twisted into incredible lilies: out at the toes, heels, tops, sides, soles. Meadow flower! ha, mallow! at last I have you. (Rot dead marigolds—an acre at a time! Gold, are you?) Ha, clouds will touch world's edge and the great pink mallow stand singly in the wet, topping reeds and—a closet full of clothes and good shoes and my-thirty-year's-master's-daughter's two cows for me to care for and a winter room with a fire in it—. I would rather feed pigs in Moonachie and chew calamus root and break crab's claws at an open fire: age's lust loose!

3

Talk as you will, say: "No woman wants to bother with children in this country";—speak of your Amsterdam and the whitest aprons and brightest doorknobs in Christendom. And I'll answer you: "Gleaming doorknobs and scrubbed entries have heard the songs of the housemaids at sun-up and—housemaids are wishes. Whose? Ha! the dark canals are whistling, whistling for who will cross to the other side. If I remain with hands in pocket leaning upon my lamppost—why—I bring curses to a hag's lips and her daughter on her arm knows better than I can tell you—best to blush and out with it than back beaten after.

In Holland at daybreak, of a fine spring morning, one sees the housemaids beating rugs before the small houses of such a city as Amsterdam, sweeping, scrubbing the low entry steps and polishing doorbells and doorknobs. By night perhaps there will be an old woman with a girl on her arm, histing and whistling across a deserted canal to some late loiterer trudging aimlessly on beneath the gas lamps.

II.

1

Why go further? One might conceivably rectify the rhythm, study all out and arrive at the perfection of a tiger lily or a china doorknob. One might lift all out of the ruck, be a worthy successor to—the man in the moon. Instead of breaking the back of a willing phrase why not try to follow the wheel through—approach death at a walk, take in all the scenery. There's as much reason one way as the other and then—one never knows—perhaps we'll bring back Euridice—this time!

Between two contending forces there may at all times arrive that moment when the stress is equal on both sides so that with a great pushing a great stability results giving a picture of perfect rest. And so it may be that once upon the way the end drives back upon the beginning and a stoppage will occur. At such a time the poet shrinks from the doom that is calling him forgetting the delicate rhythms of perfect beauty, preferring in his mind the gross buffetings of good and evil fortune.

2

Ay dio! I could say so much were it not for the tunes changing, changing, darting so many ways. One step and the cart's left you sprawling. Here's the way! and—you're hip bogged. And there's blame of the light too: when eyes are humming birds who'll tie them with a lead string? But it's the tunes they want most,—send them skipping out at the tree tops. Whistle then! who'ld stop the leaves swarming; curving down the east in their braided jackets? Well enough—but there's small comfort in naked branches when the heart's not set that way.

A man's desire is to win his way to some hilltop. But against him seem to swarm a hundred jumping devils. These are his constant companions, these are the friendly images which he has invented out of his mind and which are inviting him to rest and to disport himself according to hidden reasons. The man being half a poet is cost down and longs to rid himself of his torment and his tormentors.

3

When you hang your clothes on the line you do not expect to see the line broken and them trailing in the mud. Nor would you expect to keep your hands clean by putting them in a dirty pocket. However and of course if you are a market man, fish, cheeses and the like going under your fingers every minute in the hour you would not leave off the business and expect to handle a basket of fine laces without at least mopping yourself on a towel, soiled as it may be. Then how will you expect a fine trickle of words to follow you through the intimacies of this dance without—oh, come let us walk together into the air awhile first. One must be watchman to much secret arrogance before his ways are tuned to these measures. You see there is a dip of the ground between us. You think you can leap up from your gross caresses of these creatures and at a gesture fling it all off and step out in silver to my finger tips. Ah, it is not that I do not wait for you, always! But my sweet fellow—you have broken yourself without purpose, you are—Hark! it is the music! Whence does it come? What! Out of the ground? Is it this that you have been preparing for me? Ha, goodbye, I have a rendez vous in the tips of three birch sisters. *Encouragé vos musiciens!* Ask them to play faster. I will return—later. Ah you are kind. —and I? must dance with the wind, make my own snow flakes, whistle a contrapuntal melody to my own fuge! Huzza then, this is the dance of the blue moss bank! Huzza then, this is the mazurka of the hollow log! Huzza then, this is the dance of rain in the cold trees.

III.

1

So far away August green as it yet is. They say the sun still comes up o'mornings and it's harvest moon now. Always one leaf at the peak twig swirling, swirling and apples rotting in the ditch.

2

My wife's uncle went to school with Amundsen. After he, Amundsen, returned from the south pole there was a Scandinavian dinner, which bored Amundsen like a boyhood friend. There was a young woman at his table, silent and aloof from the rest. She left early and he restless at some impalpable delay apologized suddenly and went off with two friends, his great, lean bulk twitching agilely. One knew why the poles attracted him. Then my wife's mother told me the same old thing, how a girl in their village jilted him years back. But the girl at the supper! Ah—that comes later when we are wiser and older.

3

What can it mean to you that a child wears pretty clothes and speaks three languages or that its mother goes to the best shops? It means: July has good need of his blazing sun. But if you pick one berry from the ash tree I'd not know it again for the same no matter how the rain washed. Make my bed of witchhazel twigs, said the old man, since they bloom on the brink of winter.

There is neither beginning nor end to the imagination but it delights in its own seasons reversing the usual order at will. Of the air of the coldest room it will seem to build the hottest passions. Mozart would dance with his wife, whistling his own tune to keep the cold away and Villon ceased to write upon his Petit Testament only when the ink was frozen. But men in the direst poverty of the imagination buy finery and indulge in extravagant moods in order to piece out their lack with other matter.

IV.

1

Mamselle Day, Mamselle Day, come back again! Slip your clothes off!—the jingling of those little shell ornaments so deftly fastened—! The streets are turning in their covers. They smile with shut eyes. I have been twice to the moon since supper but she has nothing to tell me. Mamselle come back! I will be wiser this time.

That which is past is past forever and no power of the imagination can bring it back again. Yet inasmuch as there are many lives being lived in the world, by virtue of sadness and regret we are enabled to partake to some small degree of those pleasures we have missed or lost but which others more fortunate than we are in the act of enjoying.

If one should catch me in this state! —wings would go at a bargain. Ah but to hold the world in the hand then— Here's a brutal jumble. And if you move the stones, see the ants scurry. But it's queen's eggs they take first, tax their jaws most. Burrow, burrow, burrow! there's sky that way too if the pit's deep enough—so the stars tell us.

It is an obsession of the gifted that by direct onslaught or by some back road of the intention they will win the recognition of the world. Cezanne. And inasmuch as some men have had a bare recognition in their lives the fiction is continued. But the sad truth is that since the imagination is nothing, nothing will come of it. Thus those necessary readjustments of sense which are the everyday affair of the mind are distorted and intensified in these individuals so that they frequently believe themselves to be the very helots of fortune, whereas nothing could be more ridiculous than to suppose this. However their strength will revive if it may be and finding a sweetness on the tongue of which they had no foreknowledge they set to work again with renewed vigor.

2

How smoothly the car runs. And these rows of celery, how they bitter the air—winter's authentic foretaste. Here among these farms how the year has aged, yet here's last year and the year before and all years. One might rest here time without end, watch out his stretch and see no other bending than spring to autumn, winter to summer and earth turning into leaves and leaves into earth and—how restful these long beet rows—the caress of the low clouds—the river lapping at the reeds. Was it ever so high as this, so full? How quickly we've come this far. Which way is north now? North now? why that way I think. Ah there's the house at last, here's April, but—the blinds are down! It's all dark here. Scratch a hurried note. Slip it over the sill. Well, some other time.

How smoothly the car runs. This must be the road. Queer how a road juts in. How the dark catches among those trees! How the light clings to the canal! Yes there's one table taken, we'll not be alone. This place has possibilities. Will you bring *her* here? Perhaps—and when we meet on the stair, shall we speak, say it is some acquaintance—or pass silent? Well, a jest's a jest but how poor this tea is. Think of a life in this place, here in these hills by these truck farms. Whose life? Why there, back of you. If a woman laughs a little loudly one always thinks that way of her. But how she bedizens the country-side. Quite an old world glamour. If it were not for—but one cannot have everything. What poor tea it was. How cold it's grown. Cheering, a light is that way among the trees. That heavy laugh! How it will rattle these branches in six weeks' time.

3

The frontispiece is her portrait and further on—the obituary sermon: she held the school upon her shoulders. Did she. Well—turn in here then:—we found money in the blood and some in the room and on the stairs. My God I never knew a man had so much blood in his head! —and thirteen empty whisky bottles. I am sorry but those who come this way meet strange company. This is you see death's canticle.

A young woman who had excelled at intellectual pursuits, a person of great power in her sphere, died on the same night that a man was murdered in the next street, a fellow of very gross behavior. The poet takes advantage of this to send them on their way side by side without making the usual unhappy moral distinctions.

V.

1

    Beautiful white corpse of night actually! So the north-west winds of death are mountain sweet after all! All the troubled stars are put to bed now: three bullets from wife's hand none kindlier: in the crown, in the nape and one lower: three starlike holes among a million pocky pores and the moon of your mouth: Venus, Jupiter, Mars, and all stars melted forthwith into this one good white light over the inquest table,—the traditional moth beating its wings against it—except there are two here. But sweetest are the caresses of the county physician, a little clumsy perhaps—*mais*—! and the Prosecuting Attorney, Peter Valuzzi and the others, waving green arms of maples to the tinkling of the earliest ragpicker's bells. Otherwise—: kindly stupid hands, kindly coarse voices, infinitely soothing, infinitely detached, infinitely beside the question, restfully babbling of how, where, why and night is done and the green edge of yesterday has said all it could.

Remorse is a virtue in that it is a stirrer up of the emotions but it is a folly to accept it as a criticism of conduct. So to accept it is to attempt to fit the emotions of a certain state to a preceding state to which they are in no way related. Imagination though it cannot wipe out the sting of remorse can instruct the mind in its proper uses.

2

    It is the water we drink. It bubbles under every hill. How? Agh, you stop short of the root. Why, caught and the town goes mad. The haggard husband pirouettes in tights. The wolf-lean wife is rolling butter pats: it's a clock striking the hour. Pshaw, they do things better in Bangkok,—here too, if there's heads together. But up and leap at her throat! Bed's at fault! Yet—I've seen three women prostrate, hands twisted in each other's hair, teeth buried where the hold offered,—not a movement, not a cry more than a low meowling. Oh call me a lady and think you've caged me. Hell's loose every minute, you hear? And the truth is there's not an eye clapped to either way but someone comes off the dirtier for it. Who am I to wash hands and stand near the wall? I confess freely there's not a bitch littered in the pound but my skin grows ruddier. Ask me and I'll say: curfew for the ladies. Bah, two in the grass is the answer to that gesture. Here's a text for you: Many daughters have done virtuously but thou excellest them all! And so you do, if the manner of a walk means anything. You walk in a different air from the others,—though your husband's the better man and the charm won't last a fortnight: the street's kiss parried again. But give thought to your daughters' food at mating time, you good men. Send them to hunt spring beauties beneath the sod this winter,—otherwise: hats off to the lady! One can afford to smile.

3

Marry in middle life and take the young thing home. Later in the year let the worst out. It's odd how little the tune changes. Do worse—till your mind's turning, then rush into repentence and the lady grown a hero while the clock strikes.

Here the harps have a short cadenza. It's sunset back of the new cathedral and the purple river scum has set seaward. The car's at the door. I'd not like to go alone tonight. I'll pay you well. It's the kings-evil. Speed! Speed! The sun's self's a chancre low in the west. Ha, how the great houses shine—for old time's sake! For sale! For sale! The town's gone another way. But I'm not fooled that easily. *Fort sale! Fort sale!* if you read it aright. And Beauty's own head on the pillow, *à la Muja Desnuda*! *O Contessa de Alba! Contessa de Alba!* Never was there such a lewd wonder in the streets of Newark! Open the windows—but all's boarded up here. Out with you, you sleepy doctors and lawyers you,—the sky's afire and Calvary Church with its snail's horns up, sniffing the dawn—o' the wrong side! Let the trumpets blare! *Tutti i instrumenti!* The world's bound homeward.

A man whose brain is slowly curdling due to a syphilitic infection acquired in early life calls on a friend to go with him on a journey to the city. The friend out of compassion goes, and, thinking of the condition of his unhappy companion, falls to pondering on the sights he sees as he is driven up one street and down another. It being evening he witnesses a dawn of great beauty striking backward upon the world in a reverse direction to the sun's course and not knowing of what else to think discovers it to be the same power which has led his companion to destruction. At this he is inclined to scoff derisively at the city's prone stupidity and to make light indeed of his friend's misfortune.

VI.

1

Of course history is an attempt to make the past seem stable and of course it's all a lie. Nero must mean Nero or the game's up. But—though killies have green backs and white bellies, *zut!* for the bass and hawks! When we've tired of swimming we'll go climb in the ledgy forest. Confute the sages.

2

Quarrel with a purple hanging because it's no column from the Parthenon. Here's splotchy velvet set to hide a door in the wall and there—there's the man himself praying! Oh quarrel whether 'twas Pope Clement raped Persephone or—did the devil wear a mitre in that year? Come, there's much use in being thin on a windy day if the cloth's cut well. And oak leaves will not come on maples, nor birch trees either—that is provided—, but pass it over, pass it over.

A woman of good figure, if she be young and gay, welcomes the wind that presses tight upon her from forehead to ankles revealing the impatient mountains and valleys of her secret desire. The wind brings release to her. But the wind is no blessing to all women. At the same time it is idle to quarrel over the relative merits of one thing and another, oak leaves will not come on maples. But there is a deeper folly yet in such quarreling: the perfections revealed by a Rembrandt are equal whether it be question of a laughing Saskia or an old woman cleaning her nails.

3

Think of some lady better than Rackham draws them: mere fairy stuff—some face that would be your face, were you of the right sex, some twenty years back of a still morning, some Lucretia out of the Vatican turned Carmelite, some double image cast over a Titian Venus by two eyes quicker than Titian's hands were, some strange daughter of an innkeeper,—some.... Call it a net to catch love's twin doves and I'll say to you: Look! and there'll be the sky there and you'll say the sky's blue. Whisk the thing away now? What's the sky now?

By virtue of works of art the beauty of woman is released to flow whither it will up and down the years. The imagination transcends the thing itself. Kaffirs admire what they term beauty in their women but which is in official parlance a deformity. A Kaffir poet to be a good poet would praise that which is to him praiseworthy and we should be scandalized.

VII.

1

It is still warm enough to slip from the weeds into the lake's edge, your clothes blushing in the grass and three small boys grinning behind the derelict hearth's side. But summer is up among the huckleberries near the path's end and snakes' eggs lie curling in the sun on the lonely summit. But—well—let's wish it were higher after all these years staring at it deplore the paunched clouds glimpse the sky's thin counter-crest and plunge into the gulch. Sticky cobwebs tell of feverish midnights. Crack a rock (what's a thousand years!) and send it crashing among the oaks! Wind a pine tree in a grey-worm's net and play it for a trout; oh—but it's the moon does that! No, summer has gone down the other side of the mountain. Carry home what we can. What have you brought off? Ah here are thimble-berries.

In middle life the mind passes to a variegated October. This is the time youth in its faulty aspirations has set for the achievement of great summits. But having attained the mountain top one is not snatched into a cloud but the descent proffers its blandishments quite as a matter of course. At this the fellow is cast into a great confusion and rather plaintively looks about to see if any has fared better than he.

2

The little Polish Father of Kingsland does not understand, he cannot understand. These are exquisite differences never to be resolved. He comes at midnight through mid-winter slush to baptise a dying newborn; he smiles suavely and shruggs his shoulders: a clear middle A touched by a master— but he cannot understand. And Benny, Sharon, Henrietta, and Josephine, what is it to them? Yet jointly they come more into the way of the music. And white haired Miss Ball! The empty school is humming to her little melody played with one finger at the noon hour but it is beyond them all. There is much heavy breathing, many tight shut lips, a smothered laugh whiles, two laughs cracking together, three together sometimes and then a burst of wind lifting the dust again.

Living with and upon and among the poor, those that gather in a few rooms, sometimes very clean, sometimes full of vermine, there are certain pestilential individuals, priests, school teachers, doctors, commercial agents of one sort or another who though they themselves are full of graceful perfections nevertheless contrive to be so complacent of their lot, floating as they are with the depth of a sea beneath them, as to be worthy only of amused contempt. Yet even to these sometimes there rises that which they think in their ignorance is a confused babble of aspiring voices not knowing what ancient harmonies these are to which they are so faultily listening.

3

What I like best's the long unbroken line of the hills there. Yes, it's a good view. Come, let's visit the orchard. Here's peaches twenty years on the branch. Not ripe yet!? Why—! Those hills! Those hills! But you'd be young again! Well, fourteen's a hard year for boy or girl, let alone one older driving the pricks in, but though there's more in a song than the notes of it and a smile's a pretty baby when you've none other—let's not turn backward. Mumble the words, you understand, call them four brothers, strain to catch the sense but have to admit it's in a language they've not taught you, a flaw somewhere,—and for answer: well, that long unbroken line of the hills there.

Two people, an old man and a woman in early middle life, are talking together upon a small farm at which the woman has just arrived on a visit. They have walked to an orchard on the slope of a hill from which a distant range of mountains can be clearly made out. A third man, piecing together certain knowledge he has of the woman with what is being said before him is prompted to give rein to his imagination. This he does and hears many oblique sentences which escape the others.

Coda.

Squalor and filth with a sweet cur nestling in the grimy blankets of your bed and on better roads striplings dreaming of wealth and happiness. Country life in America! The cackling grackle that dartled at the hill's bottom have joined their flock and swing with the rest over a broken roof toward Dixie.

VIII.

1

Some fifteen years we'll say I served this friend, was his valet, nurse, physician, fool and master: nothing too menial, to say the least. Enough of that: so.

Stand aside while they pass. This is what they found in the rock when it was cracked open: this fingernail. Hide your face among the lower leaves, here's a meeting should have led to better things but—it is only one branch out of the forest and night pressing you for an answer! Velvet night weighing upon your eye-balls with gentle insistence; calling you away: Come with me, now, tonight! Come with me! now tonight....

In great dudgeon over the small profit that has come to him through a certain companionship a poet addresses himself and the loved one as if it were two strangers, thus advancing himself to the brink of that discovery which will reward all his labors but which he as yet only discerns as a night, a dark void coaxing him whither he has no knowledge.

2

You speak of the enormity of her disease, of her poverty. Bah, these are the fiddle she makes tunes on and it's tunes bring the world dancing to your house-door, even on this swamp side. You speak of the helpless waiting, waiting till the thing squeeze her windpipe shut. Oh, that's best of all, that's romance—with the devil himself a hero. No my boy. You speak of her man's callous stinginess. Yes, my God, how can he refuse to buy milk when it's alone milk that she can swallow now? But how is it she picks market beans for him day in, day out, in the sun, in the frost? You understand? You speak of so many things, you blame me for my indifference. Well, this is you see my sister and death, great death is robbing her of life. It dwarfs most things.

Filth and vermine though they shock the over-nice are imperfections of the flesh closely related in the just imagination of the poet to excessive cleanliness. After some years of varied experience with the bodies of the rich and the poor a man finds little to distinguish between them, bulks them as one and bases his working judgements on other matters.

3

Hercules is in Hacketstown doing farm labor. Look at his hands if you'll not believe me. And what do I care if yellow and red are Spain's riches and Spain's good blood. Here yellow and red mean simply autumn! The odor of the poor farmer's fried supper is mixing with the smell of the hemlocks, mist is in the valley hugging the ground and over Parsippany—where an oldish man leans talking to a young woman—the moon is swinging from its star.

IX.

1

Throw that flower in the waste basket, it's faded. And keep an eye to your shoes and fingernails. The fool you once laughed at has made a fortune! There's small help in a clutter of leaves either, no matter how they gleam. Punctillio's the thing. A nobby vest. Spats. Lamps carry far, believe me, in lieu of sunshine!

Despite vastness of frontiers, which are as it were the fringes of a flower full of honey, it is the little things that count! Neglect them and bitterness drowns the imagination.

2

The time never was when he could play more than mattrass to the pretty feet of this woman who had been twice a mother without touching the meager pollen of their marriage intimacy. What more for him than to be a dandelion that could chirp with crickets or do a onestep with snow flakes? The tune is difficult but not impossible to the middle aged whose knees are tethered faster to the mind than they are at eighteen when any wind sets them clacking. What a rhythm's here! One would say the body lay asleep and the dance escaped from the hair tips, the bleached fuzz that covers back and belly, shoulders, neck and forehead. The dance is diamantine over the sleeper who seems not to breathe! One would say heat over the end of a roadway that turns down hill. Cesa!

One may write music and music but who will dance to it? The dance escapes but the music, the music—projects a dance over itself which the feet follow lazily if at all. So a dance is a thing in itself. It is the music that dances but if there are words then there are two dancers, the words pirouetting with the music.

3

One has emotions about the strangest things: men—women himself the most contemptible. But to struggle with ants for a piece of meat,—a mangy cur to swallow beetles and all—better go slaughter one's own kind in the name of peace—except when the body's not there maggots swarm in the corruption. Oh let him have it. Find a cleaner fare for wife and child. To the sick their sick. For us heads bowed over the green-flowered asphodel. Lean on my shoulder little one, you too. I will lead you to fields you know nothing of. There's small dancing left for us any way you look at it.

A man who enjoyed his food, the company of his children and especially his wife's alternate caresses and tongue lashings felt his position in the town growing insecure due to a successful business competitor. Being thus stung to the quick he thinks magnanimously of his own methods of dealing with his customers and likens his competitor to a dog that swallows his meat with beetles or maggots upon it, that is, any way so he gets it.

Being thus roused the man does not seek to outdo his rival but grows heavily sad and thinks of death and his lost pleasures thus showing himself to be a person of discernment. For by so doing he gives evidence of a bastard sort of knowledge of that diversity of context in things and situations which the great masters of antiquity looked to for the inspiration and distinction of their compositions.

X.

1

If I could clap this in a cage and let that out we'd see colored wings then to blind the sun but—the good ships are anchored up-stream and the gorged seagulls flap heavily. At sea! At sea! That's where the waves beat kindliest. But no, singers are beggars or worse cannot man a ship songs are their trade. Ku-whee! Ku-whee! It's a wind in the lookout's nest talking of Columbus, whom no sea daunted, Columbus, chained below decks, bound homeward.

They built a replica of Columbus' flagship the Santa Maria and took it from harbor to harbor along the North Atlantic seaboard. The insignificance of that shell could hardly be exaggerated when comparison was made with even the very least of our present day sea-going vessels. Thus was the magnificence of enterprise and the hardihood of one Christopher Columbus celebrated at this late date.

2

You would learn—if you knew even one city—where people are a little gathered together and where one sees—it's our frontier you know—the common changes of the human spirit: our husbands tire of us and we—let us not say we go hungry for their caresses but for caresses—of a kind. Oh I am no prophet. I have no theory to advance, except that it's well nigh impossible to know the wish till after. Cross the room to him if the whim leads that way. Here's drink of an eye that calls you. No need to take the thing too seriously. It's something of a will-o-the-whisp I acknowledge. All in the pressure of an arm—through a fur coat often. Something of a dancing light with the rain beating on a cab window. Here's nothing to lead you astray. What? Why you're young still. Your children? Yes, there they are. Desire skates like a Hollander as well as runs pickaninny fashion. Really, there's little more to say than: flowers in a glass basket under the electric glare; the carpet is red, mostly, a hodge-podge of zig-zags that pass for Persian fancies. Risk a *double entendre*. But of a sudden the room's not the same! It's a strange blood sings under some skin. Who will have the sense for it? The men sniff suspiciously; you at least my dear had your head about you. It was a tender nibble but it really did you credit. But think of what might be! It's all in the imagination. I give you no more credit than you deserve, you will never rise to it, never be more than a rose dropped in the river—but acknowledge that there is, ah there is a— You are such a clever knitter. Your hands please. Ah, if I had your hands.

A woman of marked discernment finding herself among strange companions wishes for the hands of one of them and inasmuch as she feels herself refreshed by the sight of these perfections she offers in return those perfections of her own which appear to her to be most appropriate to the occasion.

3

Truth's a wonder. What difference is it how the best head we have greets his first born these days? What weight has it that the bravest hair of all's gone waiting on cheap tables or the most garrulous lives lonely by a bad neighbor and has her south windows pestered with caterpillars? The nights are long for lice combing or moon dodging—and the net comes in empty again. Or there's been no fish in this ford since Christian was a baby. Yet up surges the good zest and the game's on. Follow at my heels, there's little to tell you you'd think a stoopsworth. You'd pick the same faces in a crowd no matter what I'd say. And you'd be right too. The path's not yours till you've gone it alone a time. But here's another handful of west wind. White of the night! White of the night. Turn back till I tell you a puzzle: What is it in the stilled face of an old mender-man and winter not far off and a darky parts his wool, and wenches wear of a Sunday? It's a sparrow with a crumb in his beak dodging wheels and clouds crossing two ways.

Virtue is not to be packed in a bag and carried off to the rag mill. Perversions are righted and the upright are reversed, then the stream takes a bend upon itself and the meaning turns a livid purple and drops down in a whirlpool without so much as fraying a single fibre.

XI.

1

Why pretend to remember the weather two years back? Why not? Listen close then repeat after others what they have just said and win a reputation for vivacity. Oh feed upon petals of aedelweis! one dew drop, if it be from the right flower, is five year's drink!

Having once taken the plunge the situation that preceded it becomes obsolete which a moment before was alive with malignant rigidities.

2

When beldams dig clams their fat hams (it's always beldams) balanced near Tellus' hide, this rhinoceros pelt, these lumped stones—buffoonery of midges on a bull's thigh—invoke,—what you will: birth's glut, awe at God's craft, youth's poverty, evolution of a child's caper, man's poor inconsequence. Eclipse of all things; sun's self turned hen's rump.

3

Cross a knife and fork and listen to the church bells! It is the harvest moon's made wine of our blood. Up over the dark factory into the blue glare start the young poplars. They whisper: It is Sunday! It is Sunday! But the laws of the county have been stripped bare of leaves. Out over the marshes flickers our laughter. A lewd anecdote's the chase. On through the vapory heather! And there at banter's edge the city looks at us sidelong with great eyes,—lifts to its lips heavenly milk! Lucina, O Lucina! beneficent cow, how have we offended thee?

Hilariously happy because of some obscure wine of the fancy which they have drunk four rollicking companions take delight in the thought that they have thus evaded the stringent laws of the county. Seeing the distant city bathed in moonlight and staring seriously at them they liken the moon to a cow and its light to milk.

XII.

1

The browned trees are singing for my thirty-fourth birthday. Leaves are beginning to fall upon the long grass. Their cold perfume raises the anticipation of sensational revolutions in my unsettled life. Violence has begotten peace, peace has fluttered away in agitation. A bewildered change has turned among the roots and the Prince's kiss as far at sea as ever.

To each age as to each person its perfections. But in these things there is a kind of revolutionary sequence. So that a man having lain at ease here and advanced there as time progresses the order of these things becomes inverted. Thinking to have brought all to one level the man finds his foot striking through where he had thought rock to be and stands firm where he had experienced only a bog hitherto. At a loss to free himself from bewilderment at this discovery he puts off the caress of the imagination.

2

The trick is never to touch the world anywhere. Leave yourself at the door, walk in, admire the pictures, talk a few words with the master of the house, question his wife a little, rejoin yourself at the door—and go off arm in arm listening to last week's symphony played by angel hornsmen from the benches of a turned cloud. Or if dogs rub too close and the poor are too let your friend answer them.   much out

---

The poet being sad at the misery he has beheld that morning and seeing several laughing fellows approaching puts himself in their way in order to hear what they are saying. Gathering from their remarks that it is of some sharp business by which they have all made an inordinate profit, he allows his thoughts to play back upon the current of his own life. And imagining himself to be two persons he eases his mind by putting his burdens upon one while the other takes what pleasure there is before him.

Something to grow used to; a stone too big for ox haul, too near for blasting. Take the road round it or—scrape away, scrape away: a mountain's buried in the dirt! Marry a gopher to help you! Drive her in! Go yourself down along the lit pastures. Down, down. The whole family take shovels, babies and all! Down, down! Here's Tenochtitlan! here's a strange Darien where worms are princes.

3

But for broken feet beating, beating on worn flagstones I would have danced to my knees at the fiddle's first run. But here's evening and there they scamper back of the world chasing the sun round! And it's daybreak in Calcutta! So lay aside, let's draw off from the town and look back awhile. See, there it rises out of the swamp and the mists already blowing their sleepy bagpipes.

Often a poem will have merit because of some one line or even one meritorious word. So it hangs heavily on its stem but still secure, the tree unwilling to release it.

XIII.

1

Their half sophisticated faces gripe me in the belly. There's no business to be done with them either way. They're neither virtuous nor the other thing, between which exist no perfections. Oh, the mothers will explain that they are good girls. But these never guess that there's more sense in a sentence heard backward than forward most times. A country whose flowers are without perfume and whose girls lack modesty—the saying goes—. Dig deeper *mon ami*, the rock maidens are running naked in the dark cellars.

In disgust at the spectacle of an excess of ripe flesh that, in accordance with the local custom of the place he is in, will be left to wither without ever achieving its full enjoyment, a young man of the place consoles himself with a vision of perfect beauty.

2

I'll not get it no matter how I try. Say it was a girl in black I held open a street door for. Let it go at that. I saw a man an hour earlier I liked better much better. But it's not so easy to pass over. Perfection's not a thing you'll let slip so easily. What a body! The little flattened buttocks; the quiver of the flesh under the smooth fabric! Agh, it isn't that I want to go to bed with you. In fact what is there to say? except the mind's a queer nereid sometimes and flesh is at least as good a gauze as words are: something of that. Something of mine—yours—hearts on sleeves? Ah *zut* what's the use? It's not that I've lost her again either. It's hard to tell loss from gain anyway.

3

The words of the thing twang and twitter to the gentle rocking of a high-laced boot and the silk above that. The trick of the dance is in following now the words, *allegro*, now the contrary beat of the glossy leg: Reaching far over as if—But always she draws back and comes down upon the word flatfooted. For a moment we—but the boot's costly and the play's not mine. The pace leads off anew. Again the words break it and we both comes down flatfooted. Then—near the knee, jumps to the eyes, catching in the hair's shadow. But the lips take the rhythm again and again we come down flatfooted. By this time boredom takes a hand and the play's ended.

XIV.

1

The brutal Lord of All will rip us from each other—leave the one to suffer here alone. No need belief in god or hell to postulate that much. The dance: hands touching, leaves touching—eyes looking, clouds rising—lips touching, cheeks touching, arms about … Sleep. Heavy head, heavy arm, heavy dream—: Of Ymir's flesh the earth was made and of his thoughts were all the gloomy clouds created. Oya!

Out of bitterness itself the clear wine of the imagination will be pressed and the dance prosper thereby.

2

To you! whoever you are, wherever you are! (But I know where you are!) There's Durer's "Nemesis" naked on her sphere over the little town by the river—except she's too old. There's a dancing burgess by Tenier and Villon's *maitress*—after he'd gone bald and was shin pocked and toothless: she that had him ducked in the sewage drain. Then there's that miller's daughter of "buttocks broad and breastes high". Something of Nietzsche, something of the good Samaritan, something of the devil himself,—can cut a caper of a fashion, my fashion! Hey you, the dance! Squat. Leap. Hips to the left. Chin—ha!—sideways! Stand up, stand up *ma bonne*! you'll break my backbone. So again! —and so forth till we're sweat soaked.

Some fools once were listening to a poet reading his poem. It so happened that the words of the thing spoke of gross matters of the everyday world such as are never much hidden from a quick eye. Out of these semblances, and borrowing certain members from fitting masterpieces of antiquity, the poet began piping up his music, simple fellow, thinking to please his listeners. But they getting the whole matter sadly muddled in their minds made such a confused business of listening that not only were they not pleased at the poet's exertions but no sooner had he done than they burst out against him with violent imprecations.

3

It's all one. Richard worked years to conquer the descending cadence, idiotic sentimentalist. Ha, for happiness! This tore the dress in ribbons from her maid's back and not spared the nails either; wild anger spit from her pinched eyes! This is the better part. Or a child under a table to be dragged out coughing and biting, eyes glittering evilly. I'll have it my way! Nothing is any pleasure but misery and brokeness. THIS is the only up-cadence. This is where the secret rolls over and opens its eyes. Bitter words spoken to a child ripple in morning light! Boredom from a bedroom doorway thrills with anticipation! The complaints of an old man dying piecemeal are starling chirrups. Coughs go singing on springtime paths across a field; corruption picks strawberries and slow warping of the mind, blacking the deadly walls—counted and recounted—rolls in the grass and shouts ecstatically. All is solved! The moaning and dull sobbing of infants sets blood tingling and eyes ablaze to listen. Speed sings in the heels at long nights tossing on coarse sheets with burning sockets staring into the black. Dance! Sing! Coil and uncoil! Whip yourselves about! Shout the deliverence! An old woman has infected her blossomy grand-daughter with a blood illness that every two weeks drives the mother into hidden songs of agony, the pad-footed mirage of creeping death for music. The face muscles keep pace. Then a darting about the compass in a tarantelle that wears flesh from bones. Here is dancing! The mind in tatters. And so the music wistfully takes the lead. *Aye de mi, Juana la Loca, reina de Espagna, esa esta tu canta, reina mia!*

XV.

1

'N! cha! cha! cha! destiny needs men, so make up your mind. Here's an oak filling the wind's space. Out with him!

By carefully prepared stages come down through the vulgarities of a cupiscent girlhood to the barren distinction of this cold six A. M. Her pretty, pinched face is a very simple tune but it carries now a certain quasi-maidenly distinction. It's not at least what you'd have heard six years back when she was really virgin.

Often when the descent seems well marked there will be a subtle ascent over-ruling it so that in the end when the degradation is fully anticipated the person will be found to have emerged upon a hilltop.

2

Such an old sinner knows the lit-edged clouds. No spring days like those that come in October. Strindberg had the eyes for Swan White! So make my bed with yours, tomorrow…? Tomorrow … the hospital.

Seeing his life at an end a miserable fellow, much accustomed to evil, wishes for the companionship of youth and beauty before he dies and in exchange thinks to proffer that praise which due to the kind of life he has led he is most able to give.

3

Here's a new sort of April clouds: whiffs of dry snow on the polished roadway that, curled by the wind, lie in feathery figures. Oh but April's not to be hedged that simply. She was a Scotch lady and made her own butter and they grew their own rye. It was the finest bread I ever tasted. And how we used to jump in the hay! When he lost his money she kept a boarding house.… But this is nothing to the story that should have been written could he have had time to jot it all down: of how Bertha's lips are turned and her calf also and how she weighs 118 pounds. Do I think that is much? Hagh! And her other perfections. Ruin the girl? Oh there are fifty niceties that—being virtuous, oh glacially virtuous—one might consider, i.e. whose touch is the less venomous and by virtue of what sanction? Love, my good friends has never held sway in more than a heart or two here and there since—? All beauty stands upon the edge of the deflowering. I confess I wish my wife younger. This is the lewdest thought possible: it makes mockery of the spirit, say you? Solitary poet who speaks his mind and has not one fellow in a virtuous world! I wish for youth! I wish for love—! I see well what passes in the street and much that passes in the mind. You'll say this has nothing in it of chastity. Ah well, chastity is a lily of the valley that only a fool would mock. There is no whiter nor no sweeter flower—but once past, the rankest stink comes from the soothest petals. Heigh-ya! A crib from our mediæval friend Shakespeare.

That which is heard from the lips of those to whom we are talking in our day's-affairs mingles with what we see in the streets and everywhere about us as it mingles also with our imaginations. By this chemistry is fabricated a language of the day which shifts and reveals its meaning as clouds shift and turn in the sky and sometimes send down rain or snow or hail. This is the language to which few ears are tuned so that it is said by poets that few men are ever in their full senses since they have no way to use their imaginations. Thus to say that a man has no imagination is to say nearly that he is blind or deaf. But of old poets would translate this hidden language into a kind of replica of the speech of the world with certain distinctions of rhyme and meter to show that it was not really that speech. Nowadays the elements of that language are set down as heard and the imagination of the listener and of the poet are left free to mingle in the dance.

XVI.

1

Per le pillole d'Ercole! I should write a happy poem tonight. It would have to do with a bare, upstanding fellow whose thighs bulge with a zest for—say, a zest! He tries his arm. Flings a stone over the river. Scratches his bare back. Twirls his beard, laughs softly and stretches up his arms in a yawn. —stops in the midst—looking! A white flash over against the oak stems! Draws in his belly. Looks again. In three motions is near the stream's middle, swinging forward, hugh, hugh, hugh, hugh, blinking his eyes against the lapping wavelets! Out! and the sting of the thicket!

The poet transforms himself into a satyr and goes in pursuit of a white skinned dryad. The gaiety of his mood full of lustihood, even so, turns back with a mocking jibe.

2

Giants in the dirt. The gods, the Greek gods, smothered in filth and ignorance. The race is scattered over the world. Where is its home? Find it if you've the genius. Here Hebe with a sick jaw and a cruel husband,—her mother left no place for a brain to grow. Herakles rowing boats on Berry's Creek! Zeus is a country doctor without a taste for coin jingling. Supper is of a bastard nectar on rare nights for they will come—the rare nights! The ground lifts and out sally the heroes of Sophocles, of Æschylus. They go seeping down into our hearts, they rain upon us and in the bog they sink again down through the white roots, down—to a saloon back of the railroad switch where they have that girl, you know, the one that should have been Venus by the lust that's in her. They've got her down there among the railroad men. A crusade couldn't rescue her. Up to jail—or call it down to Limbo—the Chief of Police our Pluto. It's all of the gods, there's nothing else worth writing of. They are the same men they always were—but fallen. Do they dance now, they that danced beside Helicon? They dance much as they did then, only, few have an eye for it, through the dirt and fumes.

When they came to question the girl before the local judge it was discovered that there were seventeen men more or less involved so that there was nothing to do but to declare the child a common bastard and send the girl about her business. Her mother took her in and after the brat died of pneumonia a year later she called in the police one day. An officer opened the bedroom door. The girl was in bed with an eighteenth fellow, a young roaming loafer with a silly grin to his face. They forced a marriage which relieved the mother of her burden. The girl was weak minded so that it was only with the greatest difficulty that she could cover her moves, in fact she never could do so with success.

3

Homer sat in a butcher's shop one rainy night and smelt fresh meat near him so he moved to the open window. It is infinitely important that I do what I well please in the world. What you please is that I please what you please but what I please is well rid of you before I turn off from the path into the field. What I am, why that they made me. What I do, why that I choose for myself. Reading shows, you say. Yes, reading shows reading. What you read is what they think and what they think is twenty years old or twenty thousand and it's all one to the little girl in the *pissoir*. Likewise to me. But the butcher was a friendly fellow so he took the carcass outside thinking Homer to be no more than any other beggar.

A man's carcass has no more distinction than the carcass of an ox.

XVII.

1

Little round moon up there—wait awhile—do not walk so quickly. I could sing you a song—: Wine clear the sky is and the stars no bigger than sparks! Wait for me and next winter we'll build a fire and shake up twists of sparks out of it and you shall see yourself in the ashes, young—as you were one time.

It has always been the fashion to talk about the moon.

2

This that I have struggled against is the very thing I should have chosen—but all's right now. They said I could not put the flower back into the stem nor win roses upon dead briars and I like a fool believed them. But all's right now. Weave away, dead fingers, the darkies are dancing in Mayaguez—all but one with the sore heel and sugar cane will soon be high enough to romp through. Haia! leading over the ditches, with your skirts flying and the devil in the wind back of you—no one else. Weave away and the bitter tongue of an old woman is eating, eating, eating venomous words with thirty years mould on them and all shall be eaten back to honeymoon's end. Weave and pangs of agony and pangs of loneliness are beaten backward into the love kiss, weave and kiss recedes into kiss and kisses into looks and looks into the heart's dark—and over again and over again and time's pushed ahead in spite of all that. The petals that fell bearing me under are lifted one by one. That which kissed my flesh for priest's lace so that I could not touch it—weave and you have lifted it and I am glimpsing light chinks among the notes! Backward, and my hair is crisp with purple sap and the last crust's broken.

A woman on the verge of growing old kindles in the mind of her son a certain curiosity which spinning upon itself catches the woman herself in its wheel, stripping from her the accumulations of many harsh years and shows her at last full of an old time suppleness hardly to have been guessed by the stiffened exterior which had held her fast till that time.

3

Once again the moon in a glassy twilight. The gas jet in the third floor window is turned low, they have not drawn the shade, sends down a flat glare upon the lounge's cotton-Persian cover where the time passes with clumsy caresses. Never in this *millieu* has one stirred himself to turn up the light. It is costly to leave a jet burning at all. Feel your way to the bed. Drop your clothes on the floor and creep in. Flesh becomes so she will not even waken. And so   accustomed to the touch hours pass and not a move. The room too falls asleep and the morning's   street outside falls mumbling into a heap of black rags at seven—

Seeing a light in an upper window the poet by means of the power he has enters the room and of what he sees there brews himself a sleep potion.

XVIII.

1

How deftly we keep love from each other. It is no trick at all: the movement of a cat that leaps a low barrier. You have—if the truth be known—loved only one man and that was before my time. Past him you have never thought nor desired to think. In his perfections you are perfect. You are likewise perfect in other things. You present to me the surface of a marble. And I, we will say, loved also before your time. Put it quite obscenely. And I have my perfections. So here we present ourselves to each other naked. What have we effected? Say we have aged a little together and you have borne children. We have in short thriven as the world goes. We have proved fertile. The children are apparently healthy. One of them is even whimsical and one has an unusual memory and a keen eye. But—It is not that we have not felt a certain rumbling, a certain stirring of the earth but what has it amounted to? Your first love and mine were of different species. There is only one way for me to take up my basket of words and for you to   out. It is sit at your piano, each his own way, until I have, if it so be that good fortune smile my way, made a shrewd bargain at some fair and so by dint of heavy straining supplanted in your memory the brilliance of the old firmhold. Which is impossible. Ergo: I am a blackguard.

The act is disclosed by the imagination of it. But of first importance is to realize that the imagination leads and the deed comes behind. First Don Quixote then Sancho Panza. So that the act, to win its praise, will win it in diverse fashions according to the way the imagination has taken. Thus a harsh deed will sometimes win its praise through laughter and sometimes through savage mockery, and a deed of simple kindness will come to its reward through sarcastic comment. Each thing is secure in its own perfections.

2

After thirty years staring at one true phrase he discovered that its opposite was true also. For weeks he laughed in the grip of a fierce self derision. Having lost the falsehood to which he'd fixed his hawser he rolled drunkenly about the field of his environment before the new direction began to dawn upon his cracked mind. What a fool ever to be tricked into seriousness. Soft hearted, hard hearted. Thick crystals began to shoot through the liquid of his spirit. Black, they were: branches that have lain in a fog which now a wind is blowing away. Things move. Fatigued as you are watch how the mirror sieves out the extraneous: in sleep as in waking.

Summoned to his door by a tinkling bell he looked into a white face, the face of a man convulsed with dread, saw the laughter back of its drawn alertness. Out in the air: the sidesplitting burlesque of a sparkling midnight stooping over a little house on a sandbank. The city at the horizon blowing a lurid red against the flat cloud. The moon masquerading for a tower clock over the factory, its hands in a gesture that, were time real, would have settled all. But the delusion convulses the leafless trees with the deepest appreciation of the mummery: insolent poking of a face upon the half-lit window from which the screams burst. So the man alighted in the great silence, with a myopic star blinking to clear its eye over his hat top. He comes to do good. Fatigue tickles his calves and the lower part of his back with solicitous fingers, strokes his feet and his knees with appreciative charity. He plunges up the dark steps on his grotesque deed of mercy. In his warped brain an owl of irony fixes on the immediate object of his care as if it were the thing to be destroyed, guffaws at the impossibility of putting any kind of value on the object inside or of even reversing or making less by any other means than induced sleep—which is no solution—the methodical gripe of the sufferer. Stupidity couched in a dingy room beside the kitchen. One room stove-hot, the next the dead cold of a butcher's ice box. The man leaned and cut the baby from its stem. Slop in disinfectant, roar with derision at the insipid blood stench: hallucination comes to the rescue on the brink of seriousness: the gas-stove flame is starblue, violets back of L'Orloge at Lancy. The smile of a spring morning trickles into the back of his head and blinds the eyes to the irritation of the poppy red flux. A cracked window blind lets in Venus. Stars. The handlamp is too feeble to have its own way. The vanity of their neck stretching, trying to be large as a street-lamp sets him roaring to himself anew. And rubber gloves, the color of moist dates, the identical glisten and texture: means a ballon trip to Fez. So one is a ridiculous savior of the poor, with fatigue always at his elbow with a new jest, the newest smutty story, the prettiest defiance of insipid pretences that cannot again assert divine right—nonsensical gods that are fit to lick shoes clean: and the great round face of Sister Palagia straining to keep composure against the jaws of a body louse. In at the back door. We have been a benefactor. The cross laughter has been denied us but one cannot have more than the appetite sanctions.

3

Awake early to the white blare of a sun flooding in sidewise. Strip and bathe in it. Ha, but an ache tearing at your throat—and a vague cinema lifting its black moon blot all out. There's no walking barefoot in the crisp leaves nowadays. There's no dancing save in the head's dark. Go draped in soot; call on modern medicine to help you: the coal man's blowing his thin dust up through the house! Why then, a new step lady! I'll meet you—you know where—o' the dark side! Let the wheel click.

In the mind there is a continual play of obscure images which coming between the eyes and their prey seem pictures on the screen at the movies. Somewhere there appears to be a maladjustment. The wish would be to see not floating visions of unknown purport but the imaginative qualities of the actual things being perceived accompany their gross vision in a slow dance, interpreting as they go. But inasmuch as this will not always be the case one must dance nevertheless as he can.

XIX.

1

Carry clapping bundles of lath-strips, adjust, dig, saw on a diagonal, hammer a thousand ends fast and discover afterward the lattice-arbor top's two clean lines in a dust of dew. There are days when leaves have knife's edges and one sees only eye-pupils, fixes every catchpenny in a shop window and every wire against the sky but—goes puzzled from vista to vista in his own house staring under beds for God knows what all.

A lattice screen say fifty feet long by seven high, such a thing as is built to cut off some certain part of a yard from public view, is surprisingly expensive to put up. The wooden strips alone, if they are placed at all close together must be figured solid, as if it were a board fence. Then there are the posts, the frames, the trimming, the labor and last of all the two coats of paint. Is it a wonder the artisan cannot afford more than the luxury of these calculations.

2

Imperceptibly your self shakes free in all its brutal significance, abashed at its covered feels its subtle power renewed and breaks to the windows and draws back before the lustihood sunshine it sees there as before some imagined figure that would be there if—ah if—But for a moment your hand rests upon the palace window sill, only for a moment.

3

to be old, to put on a brown sweater. It is not It is not fair just to walk out of a November evening bare headed and with white hair in the wind. Oh the cheeks are ruddy enough and the it's not that. Worse is to ride a wheel, a grin broad enough, glittering machine that runs without knowing to move. It is no part of the eternal truth to wear white canvas shoes and a pink coat. It is a damnable lie to be fourteen. The curse of God is on her head! Who can speak of justice when young men wear round hats and carry bundles wrapped in paper. It is a case for the supreme court to button a coat in the wind, no matter how icy. Lewd to touch an arm at a crossing; the shame of it screams to the man in a window. The horrible misery brought on by the use of black shoes is more than the wind will ever swallow. To move at all is worse than murder, worse than Jack the Ripper. It's lies, walking, spitting, breathing, coughing lies that bloom, shine sun, shine moon. Unfair to see or be seen, snatch-purses work. Eat hands full of ashes, angels have lived on it time without end. Are you better than an angel? Let judges giggle to each other over their benches and use dirty towels in the anteroom. Gnaw, gnaw, gnaw! at the heads of felons.... There was a baroness lived in Hungary bathed twice monthly in virgin's blood.

A mother will love her children most grotesquely. I do not mean by that more than the term "perversely" perhaps more accurately describes. Oh I mean the most commonplace of mothers. She will be most willing toward that daughter who thwarts her most and not toward the little kitchen helper. So where one is mother to any great number of people he will love best perhaps some child whose black and peculiar hair is an exact replica of that of the figure in Velasques', Infanta Maria Theresa or some Italian matron whose largeness of manner takes in the whole street. These things relate to inner perfections which it would be profitless to explain.

XX.

1

Where does this downhill turn up again? Driven to the wall you'd put claws to your toes and make a ladder of smooth bricks. But this, this scene shifting that has clipped the clouds' stems and left them to flutter down; heaped them at the feet, so much hay, so much bull's fodder. (*Au moins*, you cannot deny you have the clouds to grasp now, *mon ami*!) Climb now? The wall's clipped off too, only its roots are left. Come, here's an iron hoop from a barrel once held nectar to gnaw spurs out of.

2

You cannot hold spirit round the arms but it takes lies for wings, turns poplar leaf and flutters off—leaving the old stalk desolate. There's much pious pointing at the sky but on the other side few know how youth's won again, the pesty spirit shed each ten years for more skin room. And who'll say what's pious or not pious or how I'll sing praise to God? Many a morning, were't not for a cup of coffee, a man would be lonesome enough no matter how his child gambols. And for the boy? There's no craft in him; it's this or that, the thing's done and tomorrow's if you push him too close, try for the another day. But butterflies, you'll have a devil at the table.

3

One need not be hopelessly cast down because he cannot cut onyx into a ring to fit a lady's finger. You hang your head. There is neither onyx nor porphyry on these roads—only brown dirt. For all that, one may see his face in a flower along it—even in this light. Eyes only and for a flash only. Oh, keep the neck bent, plod with the back to the split dark! Walk in the curled mudcrusts to one side, hands hanging. Ah well.... Thoughts are trees! Ha, ha, ha, ha! Leaves load the branches and upon them white night sits kicking her heels against the stars.

A poem can be made of anything. This is a portrait of a disreputable farm hand made out of the stuff of his environment.

XXI.

1

There's the bathtub. Look at it, caustically rejecting its smug proposal. Ponder removedly the herculean task of a bath. There's much cameraderie in filth but it's no' that. And change is lightsome but it's not that either. Fresh linen with a dab here, there of the wet paw serves me better. Take a stripling stroking chin-fuzz, match his heart against that of grandpa watching his silver wane. When these two are compatible I'll plunge in. But where's the edge lifted between sunlight and moonlight. Where does lamplight cease to nick it? Here's hot water.

It is the mark of our civilization that all houses today include a room for the relief and washing of the body, a room ingeniously appointed with water-vessels of many and curious sorts. There is nothing in antiquity to equal this.

2

Neatness and finish; the dust out of every corner! You swish from room to room and find all perfect. The house may now be carefully wrapped in brown paper and sent to a publisher. It is a work of art. You look rather askance at me. Do not believe I cannot guess your mind, yet I have my studies. You see, when the wheel's just at the up turn it glimpses horizon, zenith, all in a burst, the pull of the earth shaken off, a scatter of fragments, significance in a burst of water striking up from the base of a fountain. Then at the sickening turn toward death the pieces are joined into a pretty thing, a bouquet frozen in an ice-cake. *This* is art, *mon cher*, a thing to carry up with you on the next turn; a very small thing, inconceivably feathery.

Live as they will together a husband and wife give each other many a sidelong glance at unlikely moments. Each watches the other out of the tail of his eye. Always it seems some drunkeness is waiting to unite them. First one then the other empties some carafe of spirits forgetting that two lumps of earth are neither wiser nor sadder.... A man watches his wife clean house. He is filled with knowledge by his wife's exertions. This is incomprehensible to her. Knowing she will never understand his excitement he consoles himself with the thought of art.

3

The pretension of these doors to broach or to conclude our pursuits, our meetings,—of these papered walls to separate our thoughts of impossible tomorrows and these ceilings—that are a jest at shelter.... It is laughter gone mad—of a holiday—that has frozen into this—what shall I say? Call it, this house of ours, the crystal itself of laughter, thus peaked and faceted.

It is a popular superstition that a house is somehow the possession of the man who lives in it. But a house has no relation whatever to anything but itself. The architect feels the rhythm of the house drawing his mind into opaque partitions in which doors appear, then windows and so on until out of the vague or clearcut mind of the architect the ill-built or deftly-built house has been empowered to draw stone and timbers into a foreappointed focus. If one shut the door of a house he is to that extent a carpenter.

Coda

Outside, the north wind, coming and passing, swelling and drives it arattle against the lidless dying, lifts the frozen sand stroking the stroking the cat sit my dear and we windows cat and smiling sleepily, prrrrr.

A house is sometimes wine. It is more than a skin. The young pair listen attentively to the roar of the weather. The blustering cold takes on the shape of a destructive presence. They loosen their imaginations. The house seems protecting them. They relax gradually as though in the keep of a benevolent protector. Thus the house becomes a wine which has drugged them out of their senses.

XXII.

1

This is a slight stiff dance to a waking baby whose arms have been lying curled back above his head upon the pillow, making a flower—the eyes closed. Dead to the world! Waking is a little hand brushing away dreams. Eyes open. Here's a new world.

There is nothing the sky-serpent will not eat. Sometimes it stoops to gnaw Fujiyama, sometimes to slip its long and softly clasping tongue about the body of a sleeping child who smiles thinking its mother is lifting it.

2

Security, solidity—we laugh at them in our clique. It is tobacco to us, this side of her leg. We put it in our samovar and make tea of it. You see the stuff has possibilities. You think you are opposing the rich but the truth is you're turning toward authority yourself, to say nothing of religion. No, I do not say it means nothing. Why everything is nicely adjusted to our moods. But I would rather describe to you what I saw in the kitchen last night—overlook the girl a moment: there over the sink (1) this saucepan holds all, (2) this colander holds most, (3) this wire sieve lets most go and (4) this funnel holds nothing. You appreciate the progression. What need then to be always laughing? Quit phrase making—that is, not of course—but you will understand me or if not—why—come to breakfast sometime around evening on the fourth of January any year where eating is concerned.   you please; always be punctual

---

My little son's improvisations exceed mine: a round stone to him's a loaf of bread or "this hen could lay a dozen golden eggs". Birds fly about his bedstead; giants lean over him with hungry jaws; bears roam the farm by summer and are killed and quartered at a thought. There are interminable stories at eating time full of bizarre imagery, true grotesques, pigs that change to dogs in the telling, cows that sing, roosters that become mountains and oceans that fill a soup plate. There are groans and growls, dun clouds and sunshine mixed in a huge phantasmagoria that never rests, never ceases to unfold into— the day's poor little happenings. Not that alone. He has music which I have not. His tunes follow no scale, no rhythm—alone the mood in odd ramblings up and down, over and over with a rigor of invention that rises beyond the power to follow except in some more obvious flight. Never have I heard so crushing a critique as those desolate inventions, involved half-hymns, after his first visit to a Christian sunday school.

3

 This song is to Phyllis! By this deep snow I know it's springtime, not ring time! Good God no! The screaming brat's a sheep bleating, the rattling crib-side sheep shaking a bush. We are young! We are happy! says Colin. What's an icy room and the sun not up? This song is to Phyllis. Reproduction lets this song is! death in, says Joyce. Rot, say I. To Phyllis

---

That which is known has value only by virtue of the dark. This cannot be otherwise. A thing known passes out of the mind into the muscles, the will is quit of it, save only when set into vibration by the forces of darkness opposed to it.

XXIII.

1

Baaaa! Ba-ha-ha-ha-ha-ha-ha-ha! *Bebe esa purga*. It is the goats of Santo Domingo talking. *Bebe esa purga!* Bebeesapurga! And the answer is: *Yo no lo quiero beber!* Yonoloquierobeber!

It is nearly pure luck that gets the mind turned inside out in a work of art. There is nothing more difficult than to write a poem. It is something of a matter of slight of hand. The poets of the T'ang dynasty or of the golden age in Greece or even the Elizabethans: it's a kind of alchemy of form, a deft bottling of a fermenting language. Take Dante and his Tuscan dialect— It's a matter of position. The empty form drops from a cloud, like a gourd from a vine; into it the poet packs his phallus-like argument.

2

The red huckleberry bushes running miraculously along the except where the land's ground among the trees everywhere, tilled, these keep her from that tiredness the earth's touch lays up follows the under the soles of feet. She runs beyond the wood her laughing among the birch clusters swiftest along the roads her mouth the curls before her eyes face in the yellow leaves there where they have half open. This is a person in particular her—and I have only a wraith in the birch trees.

It is not the lusty bodies of the nearly naked girls in the shows about town, nor the blare of the popular tunes that make money for the manager. The girls can be procured rather more easily in other ways and the music is dirt cheap. It is that this meat is savored with a strangeness which never looses its fresh taste to generation after generation, either of dancers or those who watch. It is beauty escaping, spinning up over the heads, blown out at the overtaxed vents by the electric fans.

3

In many poor and sentimental households it is a custom to have cheap prints in glass frames upon the walls. These are of all sorts and many sizes and may be found in any room from the kitchen to the toilet. The drawing is always of the worst and the colors, not gaudy but almost always of faint indeterminate tints, are infirm. Yet a delicate accuracy exists between these prints and the environment which breeds them. But as if to intensify this relationship words are added. There will be a "sentiment" as it is called, a rhyme, which the picture illuminates. Many of these pertain to love. This is well enough when the bed is new and the young couple spend the long winter nights there in delightful seclusion. But childbirth follows in its time and a motto still hangs above the bed. It is only then that the full ironical meaning of these prints leaves the paper and the frame and starting through the glass takes undisputed sway over the household.

XXIV.

1

I like the boy. It's years back I began to draw him to me—or he was pushed my way by the others. And what if there's no sleep because the bed's burning; is that a reason to send a chap to Greystone! Greystone! There's a name if you've any tatter of mind left in you. It's the long back, narrowing that way at the waist perhaps whets the chisel in me. How the flanks flutter and the heart races. Imagination! That's the worm in the apple. What if it run to paralyses and blind fires, here's sense loose in a world set on foundations. Blame buzzards for the eyes they have.

Buzzards, granted their disgusting habit in regard to meat, have eyes of a power equal to that of the eagles'.

2

Five miscarriages since January is a considerable record Emily dear—but hearken to me: The Pleiades—that small cluster of lights in the sky there—. You'd better go on in the house before you catch cold. Go on now!

Carelessness of heart is a virtue akin to the small lights of the stars. But it is sad to see virtues in those who have not the gift of the imagination to value them.

Damn me I feel sorry for them. Yet syphilis is no more than a wild pink in the rock's cleft. I know that. Radicals and capitalists doing a can-can tread the ground clean. Luck to the feet then. Bring a Russian to put a fringe to the rhythm. What's the odds? Commiseration cannot solve calculus. Calculus is a stone. Frost'll crack it. Till then, there's many a good back-road among the clean raked fields of hell where autumn flowers are blossoming.

Pathology literally speaking is a flower garden. Syphilis covers the body with salmon-red petals. The study of medicine is an inverted sort of horticulture. Over and above all this floats the philosophy of disease which is a stern dance. One of its most delightful gestures is bringing flowers to the sick.

3

For a choice? Go to bed at three in the afternoon with your clothes on: dreams for you! Here's an old bonnefemme in a pokebonnet staring into the rear of a locomotive. Or if this prove too difficult take a horse-drag made of green limbs, a kind of leaf cloth. Up the street with it! Ha, how the tar clings. Here's glee for the children. All's smeared. Green's black. Leap like a devil, clap hands and cast around for more. Here's a pine wood driven head down into a mud-flat to build a school on. Oh la, la! sand pipers made mathematicians at the state's cost.

XXV.

1

There's force to this cold sun, makes beard stubble stand shinily. We look, we pretend great things to our glass—rubbing our chin: This is a profound comedian who grimaces deeds into slothful breasts. This is a sleepy president, without followers save oak leaves—but their coats are of the wrong color. This is a farmer—plowed a field in his dreams and since that time—goes stroking the weeds that choke his furrows. This is a poet left his own country—

The simple expedient of a mirror has practical use for arranging the hair, for observation of the set of a coat, etc. But as an exercise for the mind the use of a mirror cannot be too highly recommended. Nothing of a mechanical nature could be more conducive to that elasticity of the attention which frees the mind for the enjoyment of its special prerogatives.

2

A man can shoot his spirit up out of a wooden house, that is, through the roof—the roof's slate—but how far? It is of final importance to know that. To say the world turns under my feet and that I watch it passing with a smile is neither the truth nor my desire. But I would wish to stand—you've seen the kingfisher do it—where the largest town might be taken in my two hands, as high let us say as a man's head—some one man not too far above the clouds. What would I do then? Oh I'd hold my sleeve over the sun awhile to make church bells ring.

It is obvious that if in flying an airplane one reached such an altitude that all sense of direction and every intelligible perception of the world were lost there would be nothing left to do but to come down to that point at which eyes regained their power.

and oil Towels will stay in a heap—if the window's shut in a bottle—if the cork's there. But if the meat's not cut to suit it's no use rising before sun up, you'll never sweep the dust from these floors. Hide smiles among the tall glasses in the cupboard, come back when you think the trick's done and you'll find only dead flies there. It's beyond hope. You were not born of a Monday.

There are divergences of humor that cannot be reconciled. A young woman of much natural grace of manner and very apt at a certain color of lie is desirous of winning the good graces of one only slightly her elder but nothing comes of her exertions. Instead of yielding to a superficial advantage she finally gives up the task and continues in her own delicate bias of peculiar and beautiful design much to the secret delight of the onlooker who is thus regaled by the spectacle of two exquisite and divergent natures playing one against the other.

3

Hark! There's laughter! These fight and draw nearer, we—fight and draw apart. They know the things they say are true bothways, we miss the joke—try to—Oh, try to. Let it go at that. There again! Real laughter. At least we have each other in the ring of that music. "He saved a little then had to go and die". But isn't it the same with all of us? Not at all. Some laugh and laugh, with little grey eyes looking out through the chinks—but not brown eyes rolled up in a full roar. One can't have everything.

Going along an illworn dirt road on the outskirts of a mill town one Sunday afternoon two lovers who have quarreled hear the loud cursing and shouts of drunken laborers and their women, followed by loud laughter and wish that their bodies were two fluids in the same vessel. Then they fall to twitting each other on the many ways of laughing.

XXVI.

1

Doors have a back side also. And grass blades are double-edged. It's no use trying to deceive me, leaves fall more by the buds that push them off than by lack of greenness. Or throw if you think it's two shoes on the floor and see how they'll lie all one way.

2

There is no truth—sh!—but the honest truth and that is that touch-me-nots mean nothing, that daisies at a distance seem mushrooms and that—your japanese silk today was not the sky's blue but your pajamas now as you lean over the crib's edge and day's in! Grassgreen the mosquito net caught over are your head's butt for foliage. What else? except odors—an old hallway. Moresco. Salvago. —and a game of socker. I was too nervous and young to win—that day.

3

All that seem solid: melancholias, *idees fixes*, eight years at the academy, Mr. Locke, this year and the next and the next—one like another—whee!—they are April zephyrs, were one a Botticelli, between their chinks, pink anemones.

Often it happens that in a community of no great distinction some fellow of superficial learning but great stupidity will seem the most solid figure to be rooted in the earth of the place impossible to remove him. imaginable

---

XXVII.

1

The particular thing, whether it be four pinches of four divers white powders cleverly compounded to cure surely, safely, pleasantly a painful twitching of the eyelids or say a pencil sharpened at one end, dwarfs the imagination, makes logic a butterfly, offers a finality that sends us spinning through space, a fixity the mind could climb forever, a revolving mountain, a complexity with a surface of glass: the gist of poetry. D. C. al fin.

2

There is no thing that with a twist of the imagination cannot be something else. Porpoises risen in a green sea, the wind at nightfall bending the rose-red grasses and you—in your apron running to catch—say it seems to you to be your son. How ridiculous! You will pass up into a cloud and look back at me, not count the scribbling foolish that put wings to your heels, at your knees.

3

forgotten the swinging   as with the leaves Sooner or later and summer: they scurry before a wind on the branch long since frost-baked ground—have no place to rest—somehow invoke a nothing decayed: crisp not of the past burst of warm days but a summer!—neither a copse for resurrected   frost   eaters   a   summer   of   dried   leaves   undestroyed summer removed scurrying with a screech, to and fro in the half dark—twittering, chattering, scraping. Hagh!

Seeing the leaves dropping from the high and low branches the thought rises: this day of all others is the one chosen, all other days fall away from it on either side and only itself remains in perfect fulness. It is its own summer, of its leaves as they scrape on the smooth ground it must build its perfection. The gross summer of the year is only a halting counterpart of those fiery days of secret triumph which in reality themselves paint the year as if upon a parchment, giving each season a mockery of the warmth or frozeness which is within ourselves. The true seasons blossom or wilt not in fixed order but so that many of them may pass in a few weeks or hours whereas sometimes a whole life passes and the season remains of a piece from one end to the other.

THE END.

Milton Keynes UK
Ingram Content Group UK Ltd.
UKHW042002041223
433765UK00008B/920